GRAPHIC BIOGRAPHIES

JOHN F. KENNEDY

American ☆ Visionary

by Nathan Olson

illustrated by Brian Bascle

Consultant:
Robert E. Gilbert, PhD
Professor of Political Science
Northeastern University
Boston, Massachusetts

Capstone
press

Mankato, Minnesota

Graphic Library is published by Capstone Press,
151 Good Counsel Drive, P.O. Box 669, Mankato, Minnesota 56002.
www.capstonepress.com

Printed in the United States of America

1 2 3 4 5 6 12 11 10 09 08 07

Library of Congress Cataloging-in-Publication Data
Olson, Nathan.
John F. Kennedy : American visionary / by Nathan Olson; illustrated by Brian Bascle.
p. cm.—(Graphic library. Graphic biographies)
Includes bibliographical references and index.
Audience: Grades 4-6.
ISBN-13: 978-0-7368-6852-5 (hardcover)
ISBN-10: 0-7368-6852-6 (hardcover)
ISBN-13: 978-0-7368-7904-0 (softcover pbk.)
ISBN-10: 0-7368-7904-8 (softcover pbk.)
1. Kennedy, John F. (John Fitzgerald), 1917–1963—Juvenile literature. 2. Presidents—United States—Biography—Juvenile literature. 3. Graphic novels. I. Bascle, Brian, ill. II. Title. III. Series.
E842.Z9O47 2007
973.922092—dc22
[B] 2006023333

Summary: In graphic novel format, tells the story of John F. Kennedy, the youngest elected U.S. president who is remembered for his lasting impact on civil rights, foreign policy, and the space program.

Designer
Alison Thiele

Editor
Christine Peterson

Editor's note: Direct quotations from primary sources are indicated by a yellow background.

Direct quotations appear on the following pages:

Page 10, quote attributed to John F. Kennedy; page 14, acceptance speech by John F. Kennedy at the Democratic National Convention on July 15, 1960; page 15, from transcripts of the first Kennedy-Nixon debate on September 26, 1960; page 16, from Kennedy's inaugural address on January 20, 1961; page 19, from Kennedy's speech to Congress on May 25, 1961; page 23, from Kennedy's speech in Berlin on June 26, 1963; as documented at the John F. Kennedy Presidential Library and Museum in Boston, Massachusetts (http://www.jfklibrary.org).

Page 11, quote attributed to Joseph Kennedy Jr., as published in *An Unfinished Life: John F. Kennedy 1917–1963* by Robert Dallek (Boston: Little, Brown, and Co., 2003).

Page 22, from Martin Luther King Jr.'s letter from the Birmingham Jail, April 1963; page 23, from King's "I Have a Dream" speech on August 28, 1963; as recorded by the Martin Luther King Jr. Papers Project at Stanford University (http://www.stanford.edu/group/King/mlkpapers).

Table of Contents

Chapter 1
THE SECOND SON

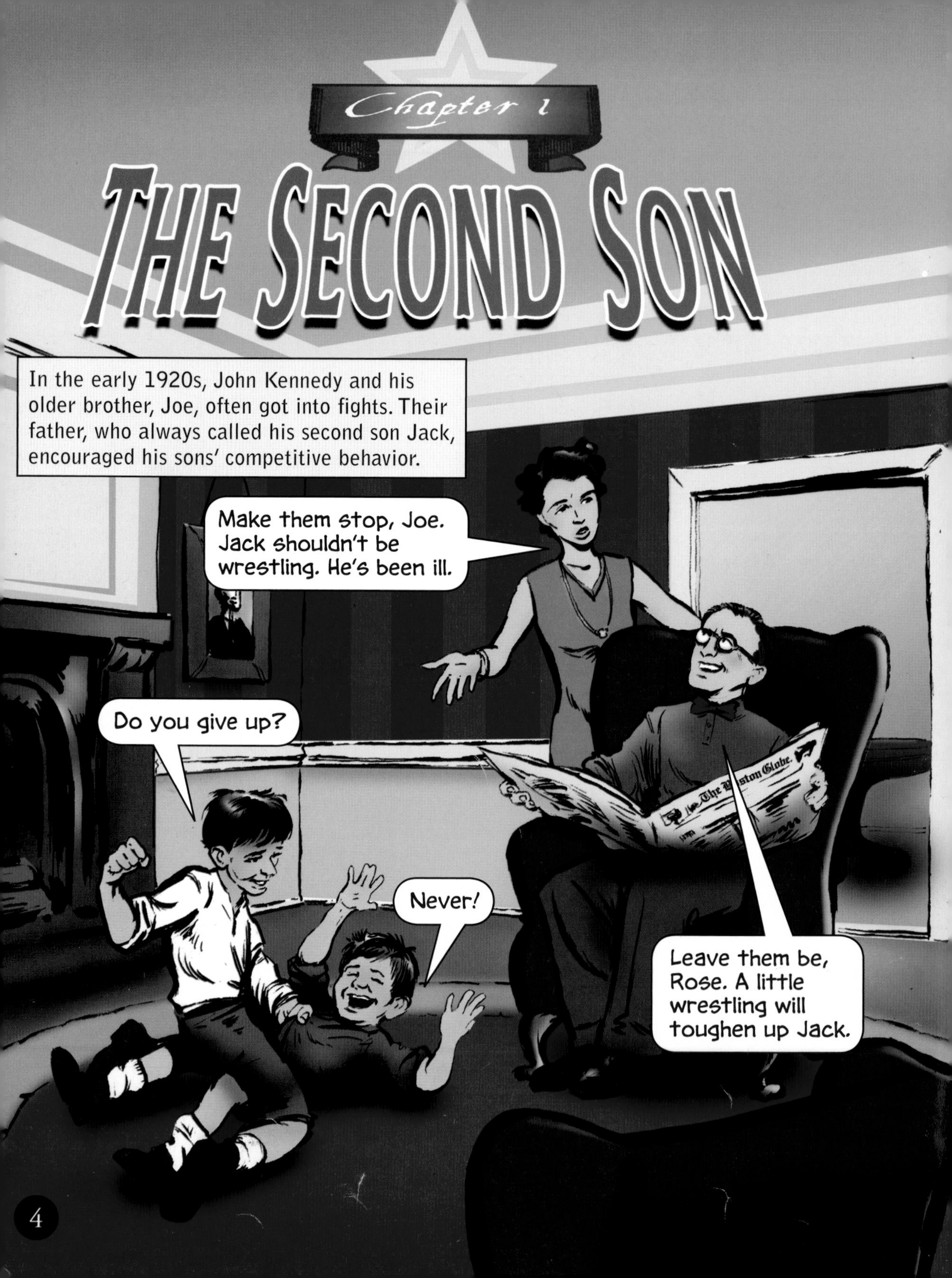

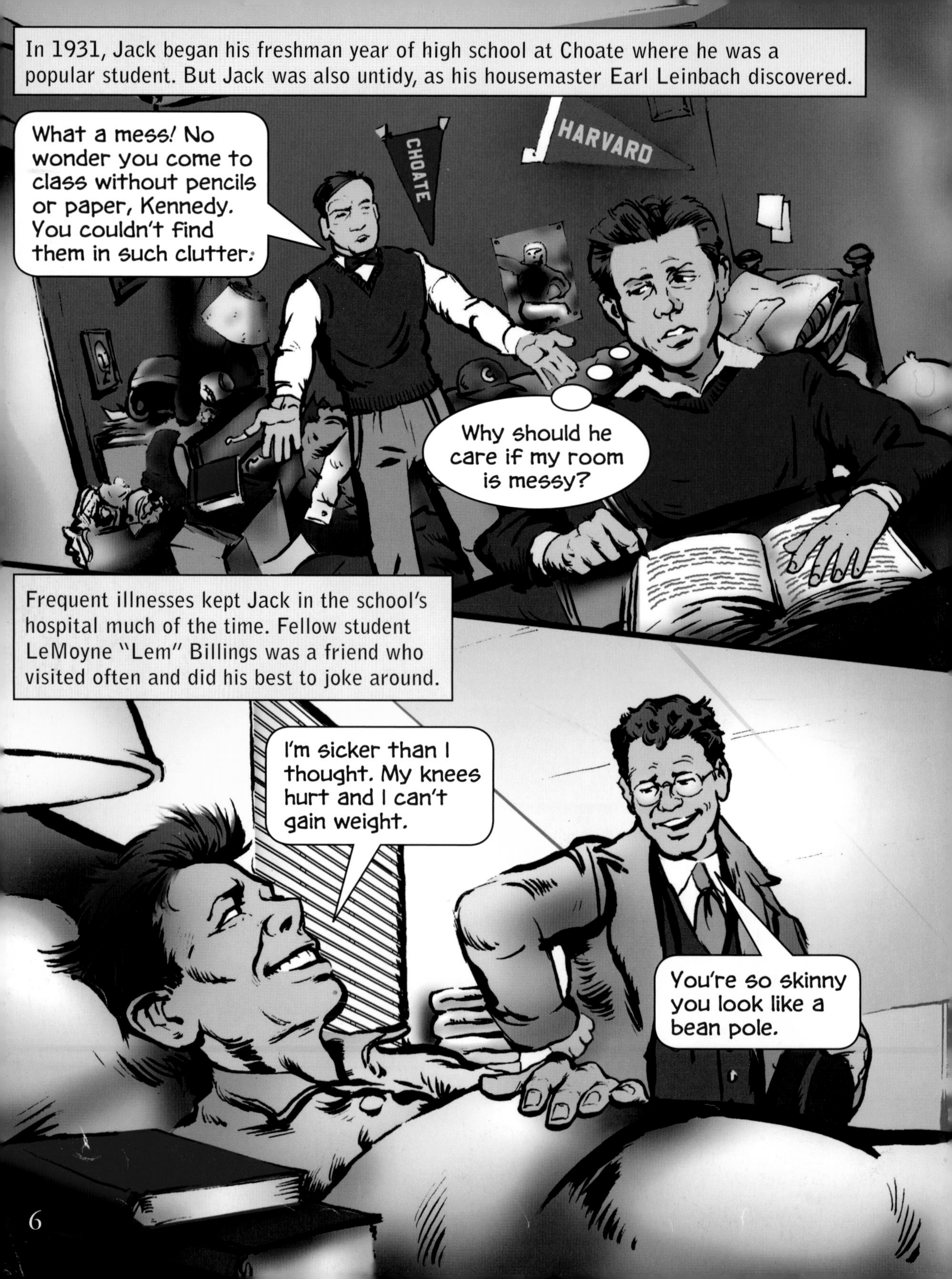
In 1931, Jack began his freshman year of high school at Choate where he was a popular student. But Jack was also untidy, as his housemaster Earl Leinbach discovered.
HARVARD
CHOATE
What a mess! No wonder you come to class without pencils or paper, Kennedy. You couldn't find them in such clutter.
Why should he care if my room is messy?
Frequent illnesses kept Jack in the school's hospital much of the time. Fellow student LeMoyne "Lem" Billings was a friend who visited often and did his best to joke around.
I'm sicker than I thought. My knees hurt and I can't gain weight.
You're so skinny you look like a bean pole.

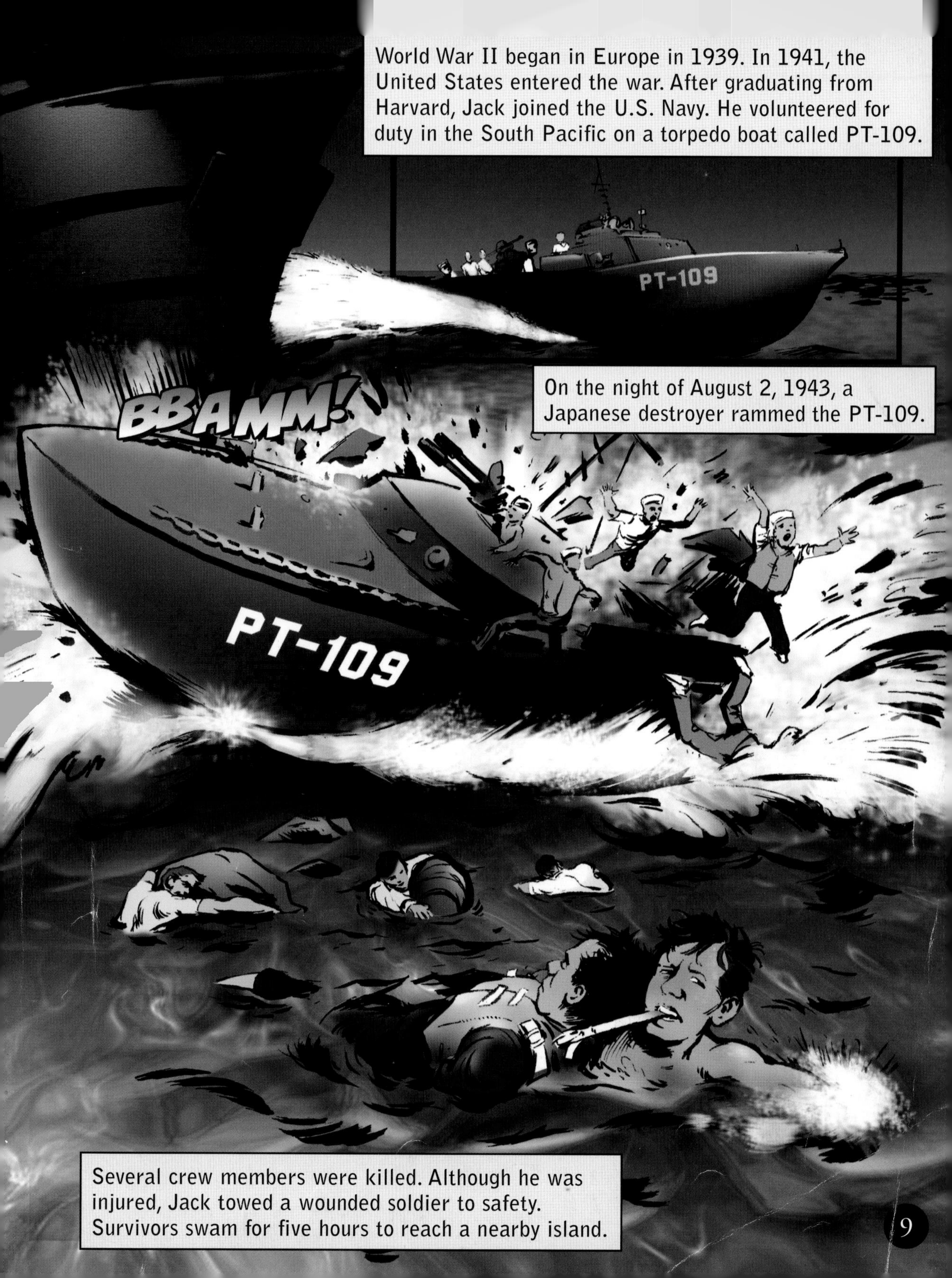
World War II began in Europe in 1939. In 1941, the United States entered the war. After graduating from Harvard, Jack joined the U.S. Navy. He volunteered for duty in the South Pacific on a torpedo boat called PT-109.
PT-109
On the night of August 2, 1943, a Japanese destroyer rammed the PT-109.
BBAMM!
PT-109
Several crew members were killed. Although he was injured, Jack towed a wounded soldier to safety. Survivors swam for five hours to reach a nearby island.

Chapter 2

ROAD TO THE WHITE HOUSE

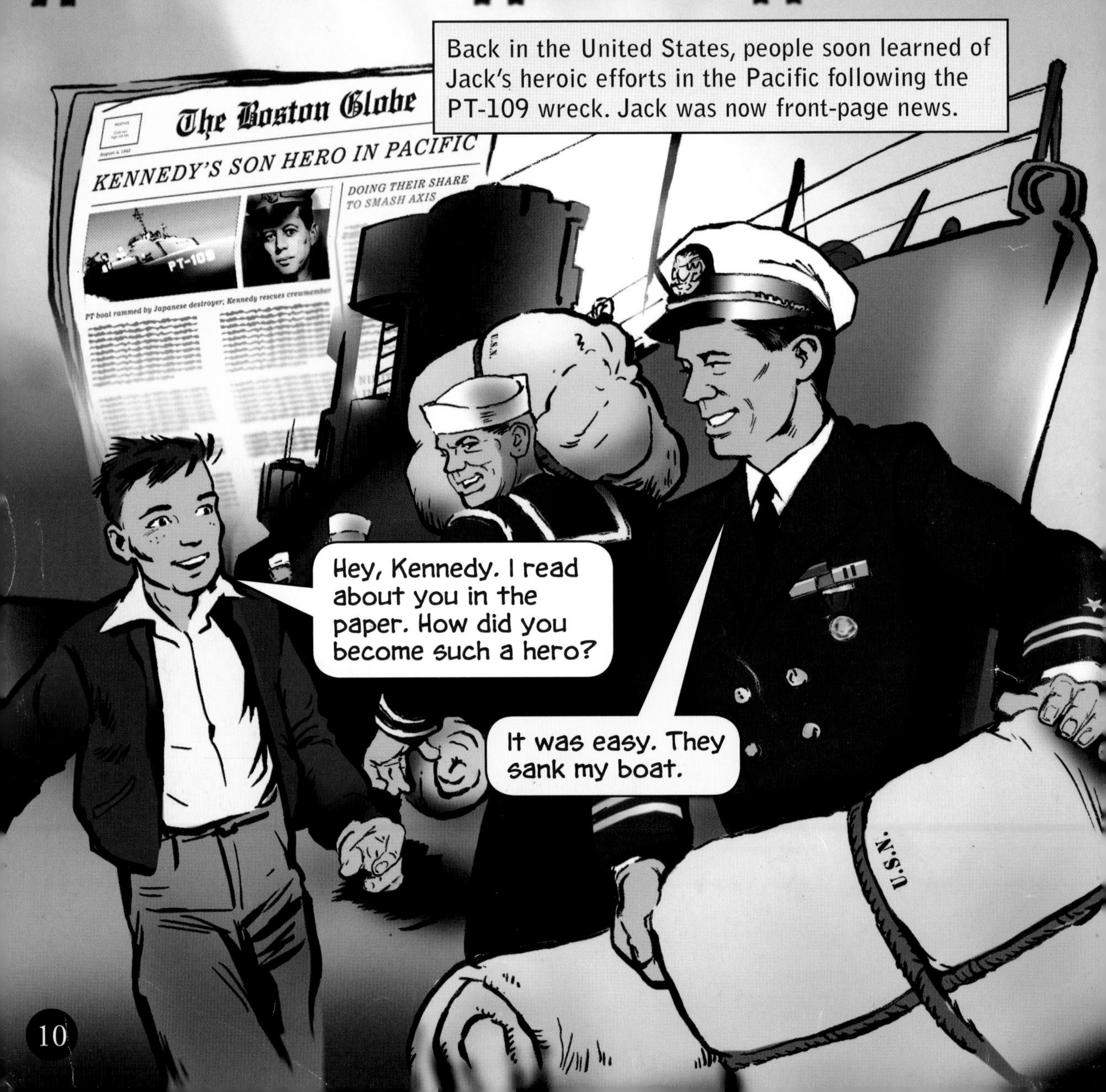

Back in the United States, people soon learned of Jack's heroic efforts in the Pacific following the PT-109 wreck. Jack was now front-page news.
The Boston Globe
KENNEDY'S SON HERO IN PACIFIC
DOING THEIR SHARE TO SMASH AXIS
PT-109
PT boat rammed by Japanese destroyer; Kennedy rescues crewmember
U.S.N.
Hey, Kennedy. I read about you in the paper. How did you become such a hero?
It was easy. They sank my boat.
U.S.N.

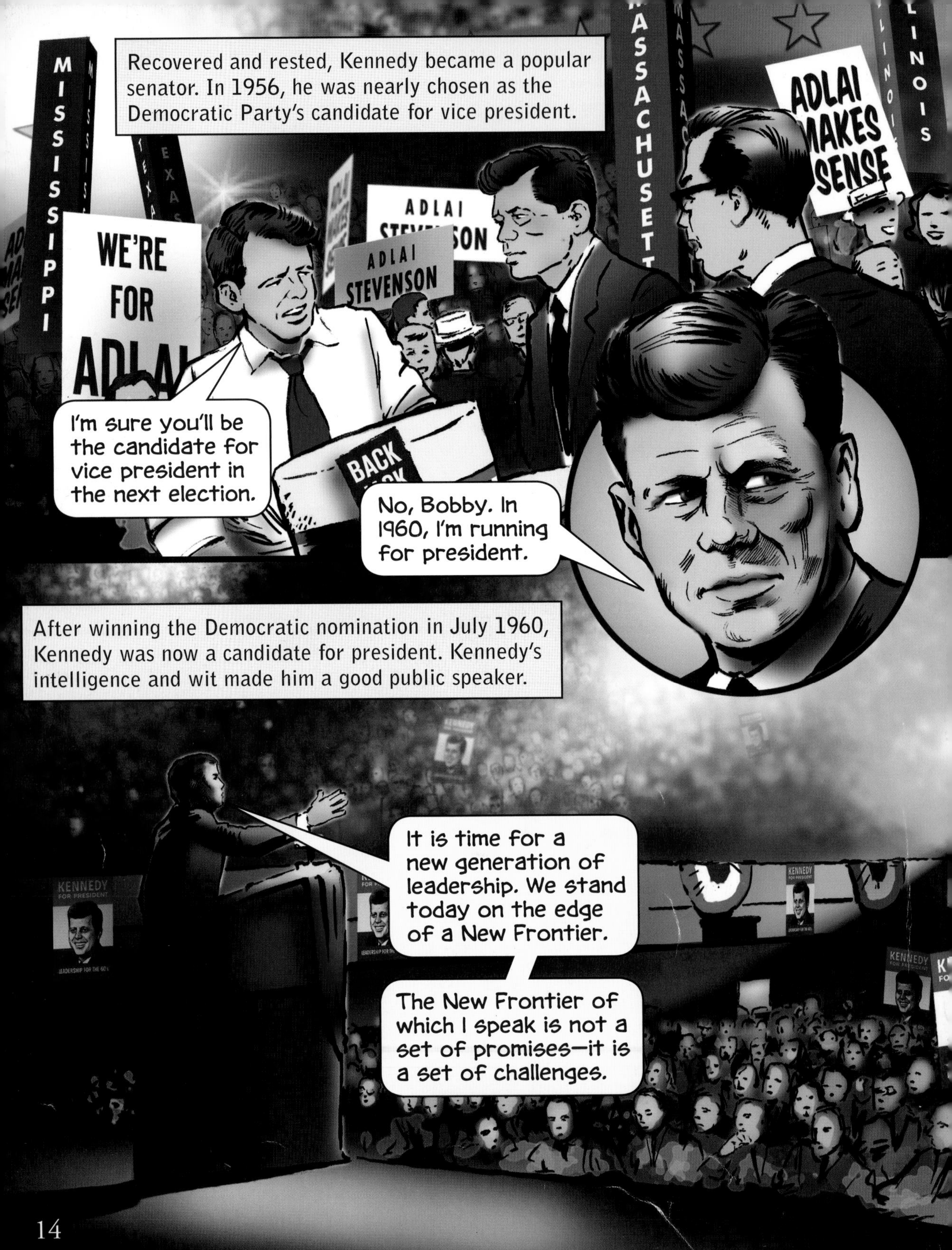
Recovered and rested, Kennedy became a popular senator. In 1956, he was nearly chosen as the Democratic Party's candidate for vice president.
MISSISSIPPI
TEXAS
WE'RE FOR ADLAI
ADLAI STEVENSON
ADLAI MAKES SENSE
MASSACHUSETTS
ILLINOIS
I'm sure you'll be the candidate for vice president in the next election.
BACK
No, Bobby. In 1960, I'm running for president.
After winning the Democratic nomination in July 1960, Kennedy was now a candidate for president. Kennedy's intelligence and wit made him a good public speaker.
KENNEDY FOR PRESIDENT
It is time for a new generation of leadership. We stand today on the edge of a New Frontier.
The New Frontier of which I speak is not a set of promises—it is a set of challenges.

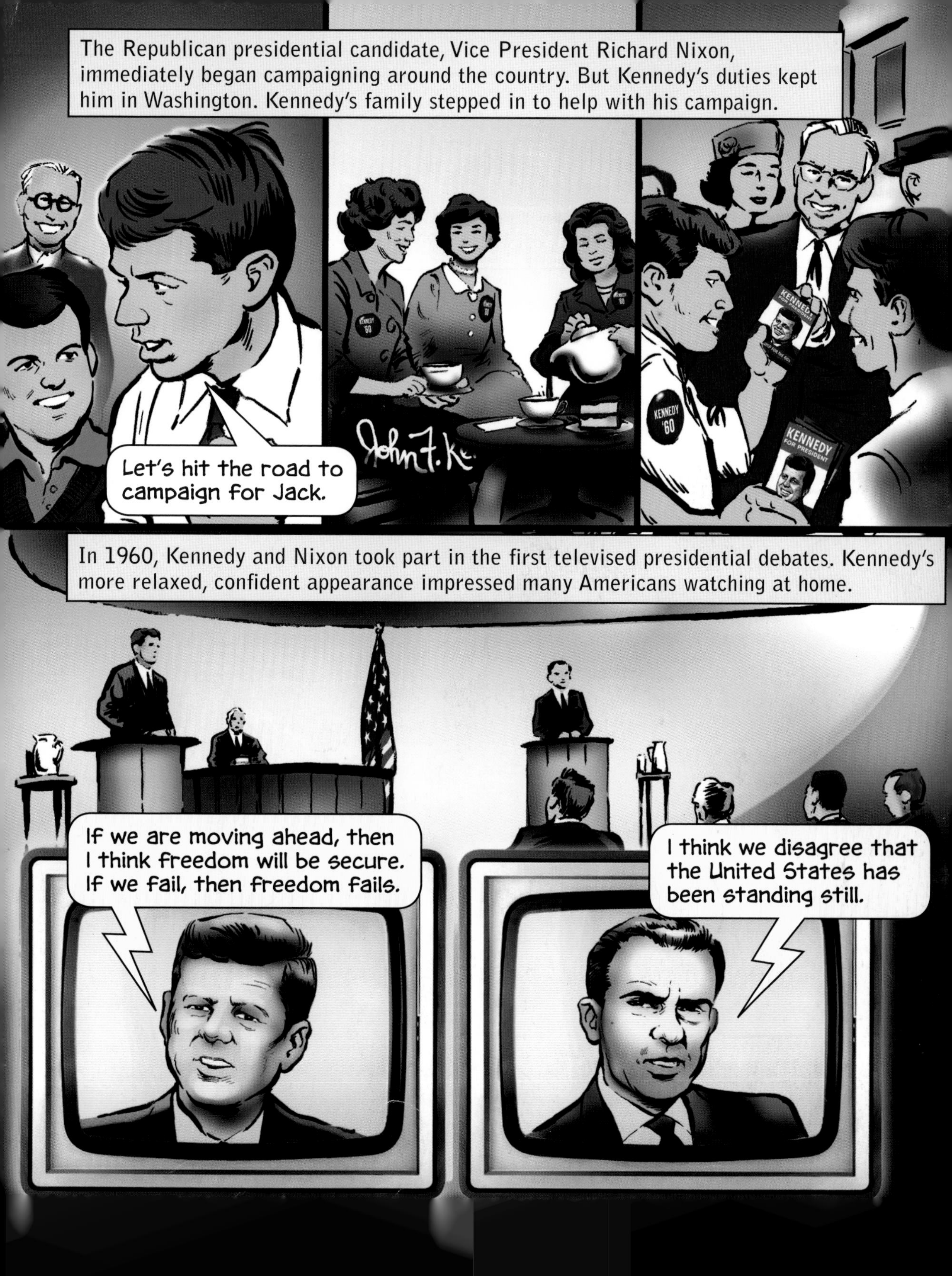
The Republican presidential candidate, Vice President Richard Nixon, immediately began campaigning around the country. But Kennedy's duties kept him in Washington. Kennedy's family stepped in to help with his campaign.
Let's hit the road to campaign for Jack.
KENNEDY '60
KENNEDY FOR PRESIDENT
In 1960, Kennedy and Nixon took part in the first televised presidential debates. Kennedy's more relaxed, confident appearance impressed many Americans watching at home.
If we are moving ahead, then I think freedom will be secure. If we fail, then freedom fails.
I think we disagree that the United States has been standing still.

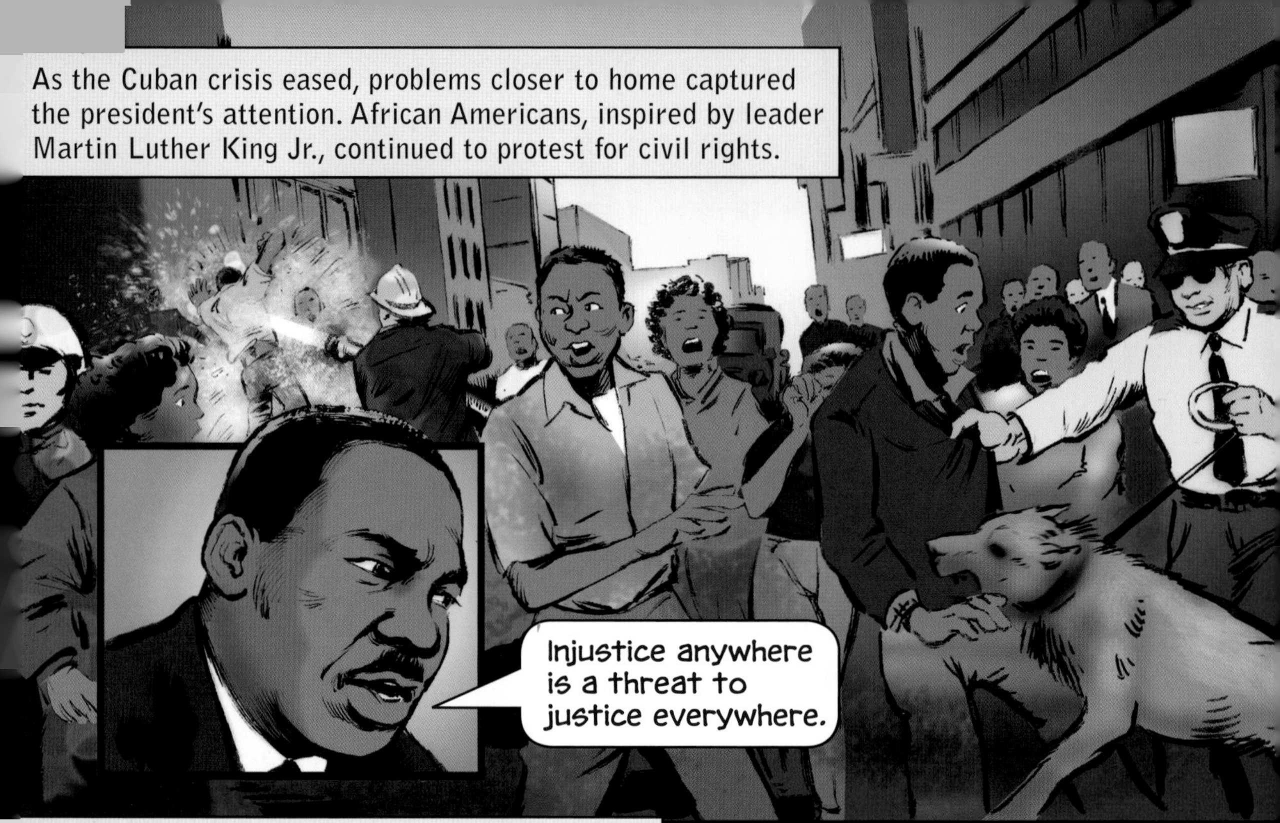
As the Cuban crisis eased, problems closer to home captured the president's attention. African Americans, inspired by leader Martin Luther King Jr., continued to protest for civil rights.
Injustice anywhere is a threat to justice everywhere.

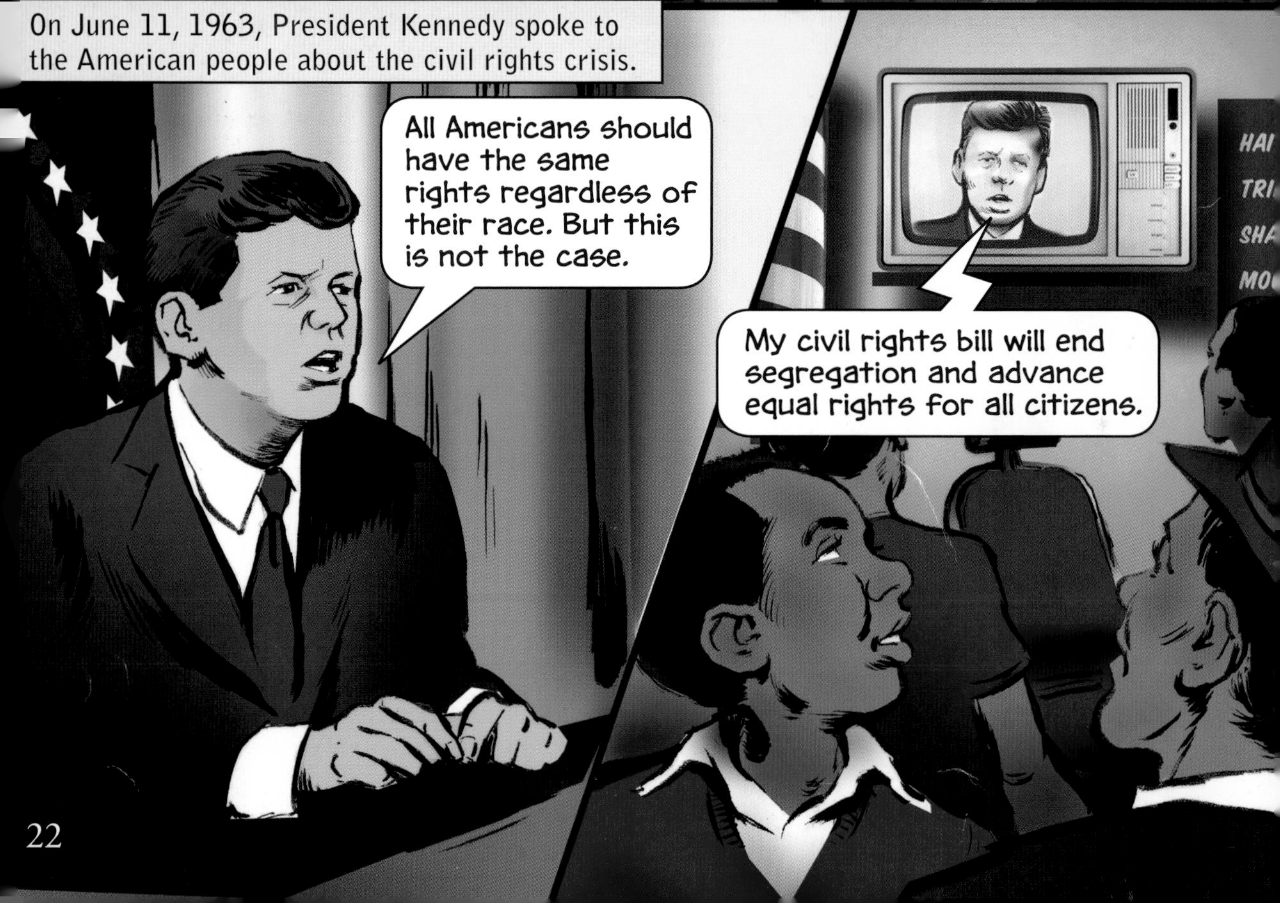
On June 11, 1963, President Kennedy spoke to the American people about the civil rights crisis.
All Americans should have the same rights regardless of their race. But this is not the case.
My civil rights bill will end segregation and advance equal rights for all citizens.

Chapter 4

THE JFK LEGACY

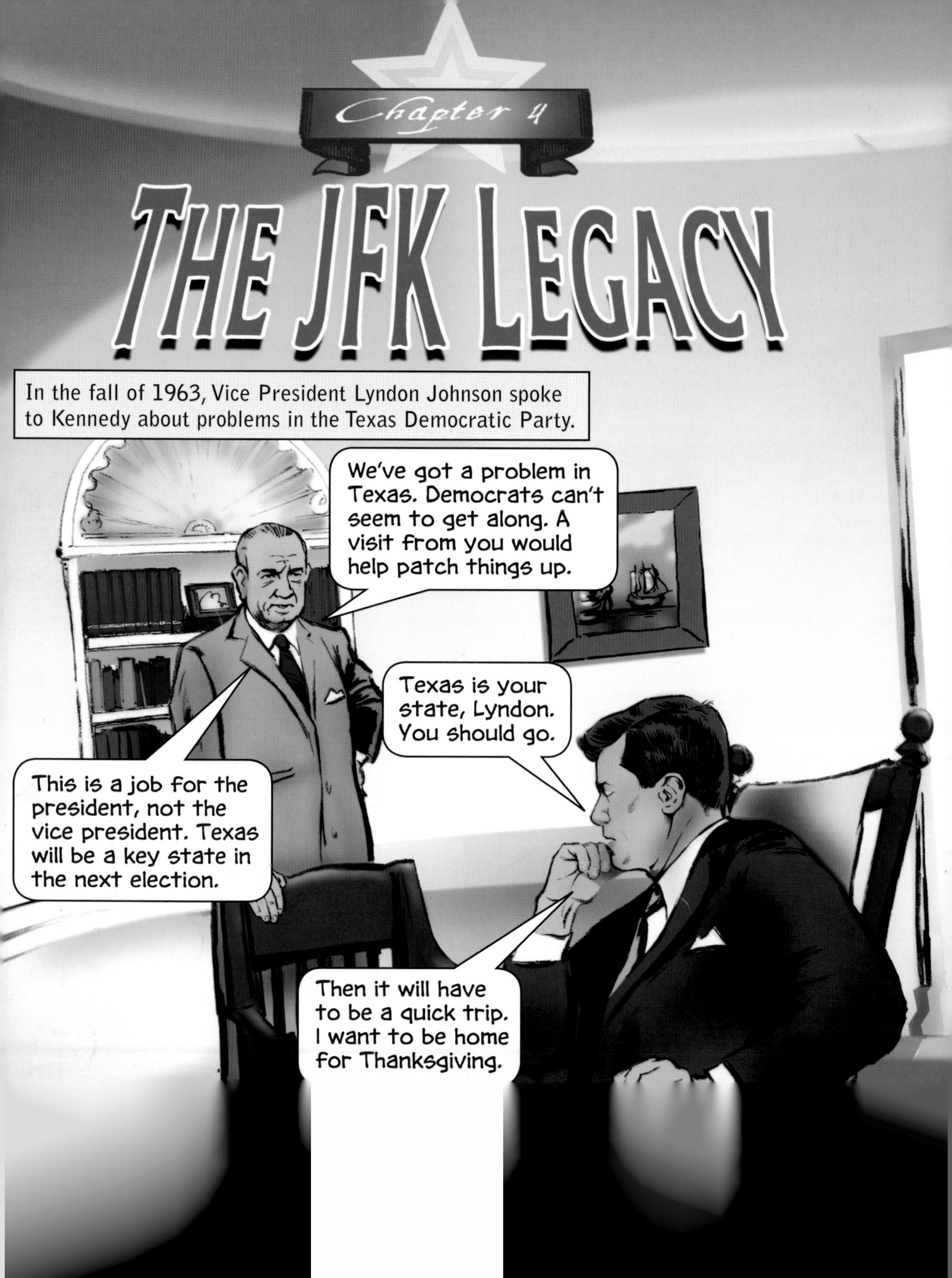
In the fall of 1963, Vice President Lyndon Johnson spoke to Kennedy about problems in the Texas Democratic Party.
We've got a problem in Texas. Democrats can't seem to get along. A visit from you would help patch things up.
Texas is your state, Lyndon. You should go.
This is a job for the president, not the vice president. Texas will be a key state in the next election.
Then it will have to be a quick trip. I want to be home for Thanksgiving.

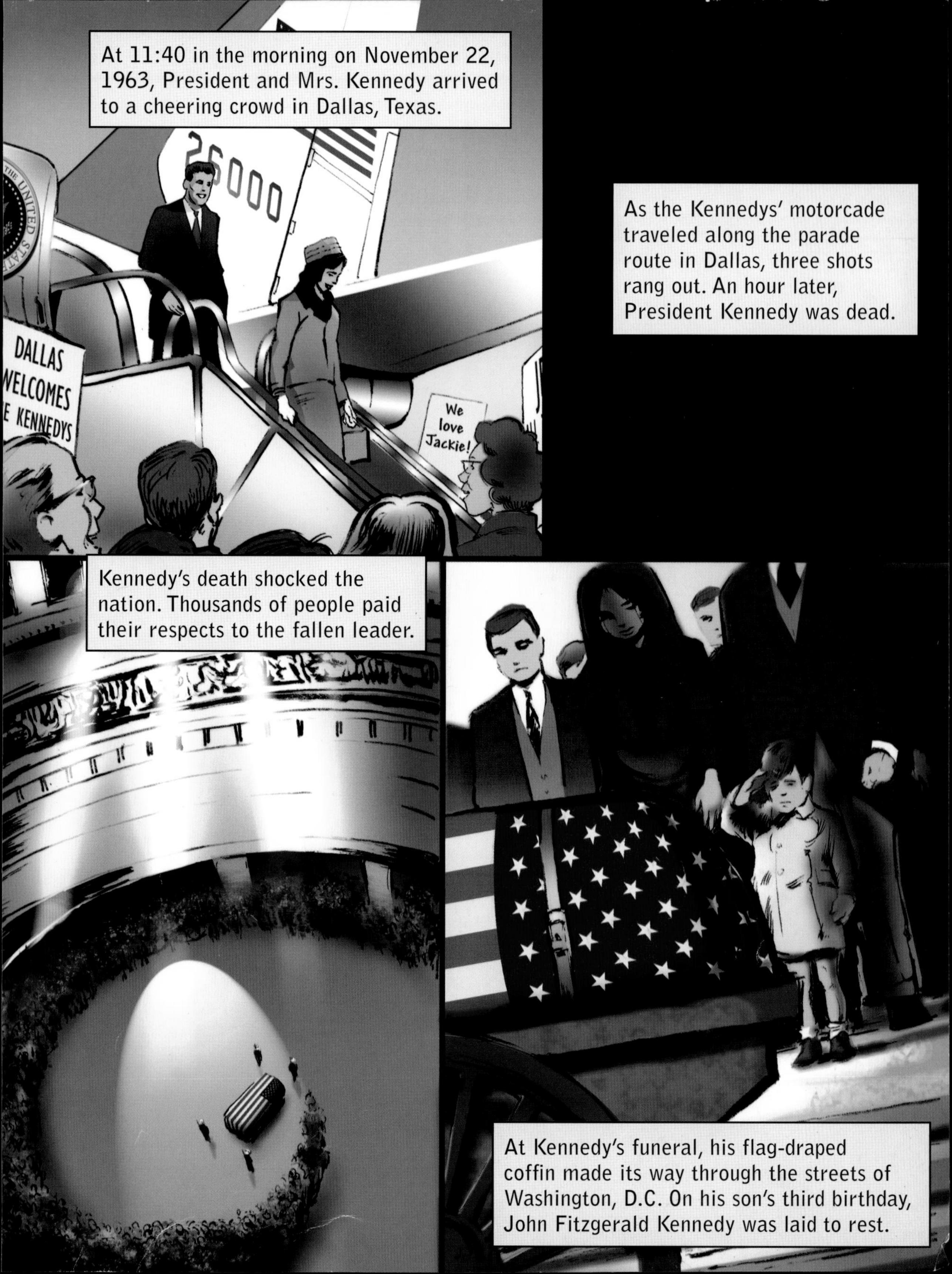

At 11:40 in the morning on November 22, 1963, President and Mrs. Kennedy arrived to a cheering crowd in Dallas, Texas.
26000
DALLAS
We love Jackie!
As the Kennedys' motorcade traveled along the parade route in Dallas, three shots rang out. An hour later, President Kennedy was dead.
Kennedy's death shocked the nation. Thousands of people paid their respects to the fallen leader.
At Kennedy's funeral, his flag-draped coffin made its way through the streets of Washington, D.C. On his son's third birthday, John Fitzgerald Kennedy was laid to rest.

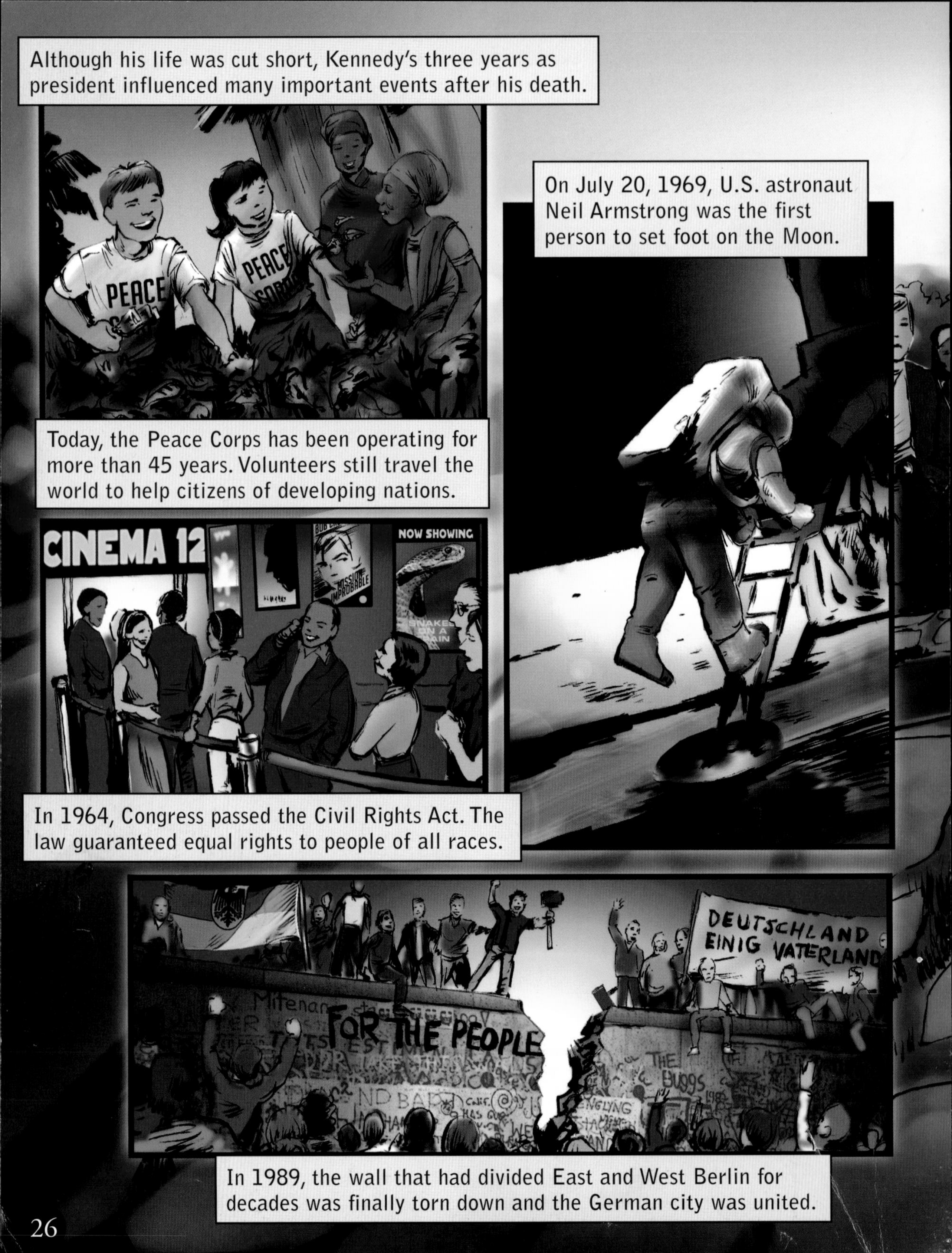
Although his life was cut short, Kennedy's three years as president influenced many important events after his death.
PEACE
PEACE
Today, the Peace Corps has been operating for more than 45 years. Volunteers still travel the world to help citizens of developing nations.
CINEMA 12
NOW SHOWING
MISSION IMPROBABLE
In 1964, Congress passed the Civil Rights Act. The law guaranteed equal rights to people of all races.
On July 20, 1969, U.S. astronaut Neil Armstrong was the first person to set foot on the Moon.
FOR THE PEOPLE
DEUTSCHLAND EINIG VATERLAND
In 1989, the wall that had divided East and West Berlin for decades was finally torn down and the German city was united.

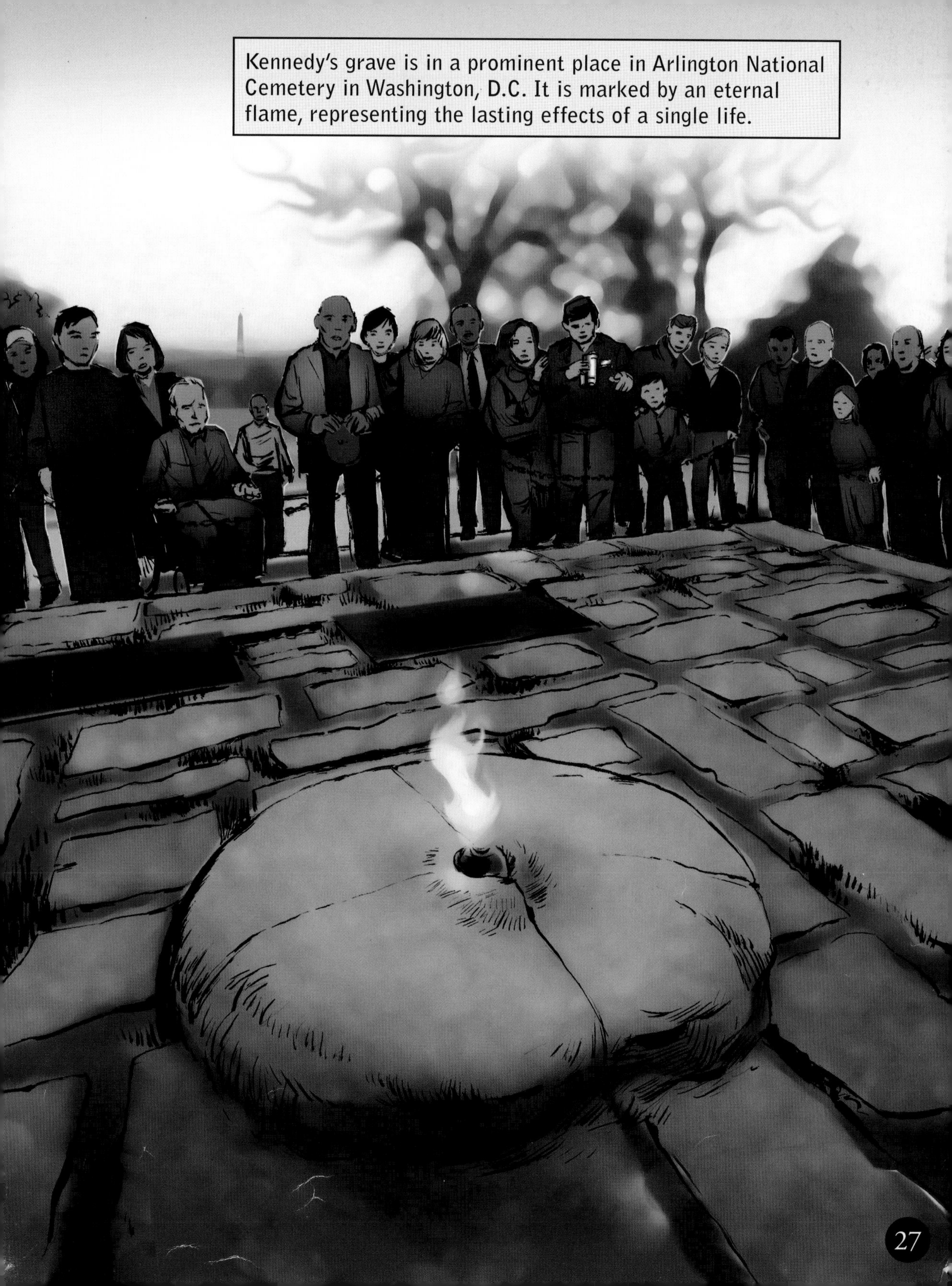
Kennedy's grave is in a prominent place in Arlington National Cemetery in Washington, D.C. It is marked by an eternal flame, representing the lasting effects of a single life.

JOHN F. KENNEDY

 John Fitzgerald Kennedy was born May 29, 1917, in Brookline, Massachusetts. He died November 22, 1963, in Dallas, Texas.

 Kennedy was the youngest man ever to be elected U.S. president. He was also the youngest president to die while in office.

 Kennedy's middle name, Fitzgerald, was in honor of his mother's father, John Francis Fitzgerald. Once Kennedy was elected president, newspapers began referring to him as JFK. His initials took up less space in headlines than his name.

 When Kennedy was a student at Choate, he was briefly expelled for one of his many pranks. He was able to return to school and graduated 65th out of a class of 110 students. His friends named him "Most Likely to Succeed."

 Kennedy and his wife, Jackie, had their first child, Caroline, on November 27, 1957. Their second child, John Jr., was born November 25, 1960. The couple's second son and third child, Patrick, was born August 7, 1963. He died two days later.

After the first Kennedy-Nixon debate, people had different opinions on who won the debate. People who listened to the debate on the radio believed Nixon had done a better job. But people who watched the event on TV thought Kennedy won the debate.

 Throughout his life, Kennedy had a number of medical problems including severe back pain and Addison's disease, which affects the body's adrenal glands. Kennedy wore a back brace throughout his presidency. He found that sitting in a rocking chair was most comfortable.

 Who fired the bullet that killed President Kennedy? Dallas police arrested Lee Harvey Oswald for the president's murder. Oswald was shot and killed by Jack Ruby while in police custody. Many people, however, believed that several gunmen were involved in a plan to kill Kennedy. Officially, Oswald is considered to be the only gunman, shooting from a sixth floor window of the Texas School Book Depository. Today, the sixth floor of this building is a museum devoted to the events of November 22, 1963.

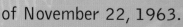

29

GLOSSARY

assure (uh-SHUR)—to promise something

blockade (blok-ADE)—a closing off of an area to keep people or supplies from going in or out

communism (KOM-yuh-niz-uhm)—a way of organizing a country so that all the land, houses, and factories belong to the government, and the profits are shared by all

crisis (KRYE-siss)—a time of danger and difficulty

diplomatic (dip-luh-MAT-ik)—being good at dealing with people

quarantine (KWOR-uhn-teen)—the act of keeping others away from a certain area

Soviet Union (SOH-vee-et YOON-yuhn)—a former federation of 15 republics that included Russia, Ukraine, and other nations of eastern Europe and northern Asia; also called the Union of Soviet Socialist Republics (USSR).

INTERNET SITES

FactHound offers a safe, fun way to find Internet sites related to this book. All of the sites on FactHound have been researched by our staff.

Here's how:
1. Visit *www.facthound.com*
2. Choose your grade level.
3. Type in this book ID **0736868526** for age-appropriate sites. You may also browse subjects by clicking on letters, or by clicking on pictures and words.
4. Click on the **Fetch It** button.

FactHound will fetch the best sites for you!

READ MORE

Ashby, Ruth. *John and Jacqueline Kennedy.* Presidents and First Ladies. Milwaukee: World Almanac Library, 2005.

Byrne, Paul J. *The Cuban Missile Crisis: To the Brink of War.* Snapshots in History. Minneapolis: Compass Point Books, 2006.

Kaplan, Howard S. *John F. Kennedy.* DK Biography. New York: DK Publishing, 2004.

Supples, Kevin. *The Civil Rights Movement.* People Who Changed America. Washington, D.C.: National Geographic Society, 2003.

BIBLIOGRAPHY

Dallek, Robert. *An Unfinished Life: John F. Kennedy 1917–1963.* Boston: Little, Brown, and Co., 2003.

Gilbert, Robert E. *The Mortal Presidency: Illness and Anguish in the White House.* New York: Fordham University Press, 1998.

Kennedy, John F. *Profiles in Courage.* New York: Harper, 1956.

O'Brien, Michael. *John F. Kennedy: A Biography.* New York: Thomas Dunne Books/St. Martin's Press, 2005.

INDEX